BEHIND THE WORSHIP

A 40-DAY DEVOTIONAL FOR TODAY'S MUSICAL WORSHIP LEADER

NIA ANDERSON

PREFACE

Serving as a musical worship leader in the church remains a significant part of the health and vitality of the church. It doesn't need to be said that a person must be called by God to perform such a task, because it is so much more than the ability to hold a tune or read music. When you look through Nehemiah in the Old Testament, the role of the "singers" is held in high regard; they had a high position in Jewish society (11:22; 12:45), and were therefore held to a higher standard of living.

In times like these, it is important for you and me to make every note intentional so the people of God will be comforted, compelled, challenged, and even convicted. Ultimately, we are leading them – whether we are in a church of twenty or twenty thousand – to the face of God, preparing them to receive the Word of God. We possess a critical role that we shouldn't take lightly: We are responsible for making the presence of God known. His Spirit is already there in the church, being that we are in His house among His people, though not every person will recognize Him. That's where we come in. This devotional therefore seeks to encourage musical worship leaders to foster their personal worship before they lead people in worship musically.

Musical worship leading is a true passion and joy of mine, and as I have grown over the last several years in my calling and gift as a worship leader, I have seen many devotionals for all kinds of people, but not as many as I expected for musical worship leaders. While leading devotions with a youth group a few years ago, I took it upon myself to create a full devotional catalogue. The end product of that catalogue is what you're holding now, and I pray it will inspire and encourage musical worship leaders – those who recently accepted the calling and those who have been leading longer than I have been alive. I pray you just don't go through the motions based on tradition or what is considered normal as it relates to leading a congregation in song, but instead choose to take your place in the Kingdom of God.

Each verse has been carefully selected for each daily lesson, and a space for journaling is provided below each lesson for you to write notes, thoughts, or whatever speaks to you. My prayer is that you will make your way through this devotional and realize your incredible calling, should you actually be called to such a position, and be strengthened and more deliberate in the way the Lord will have you to lead His people in this manner.

BEHIND THE WORSHIP

DAY 1

Speak to one another with psalms, hymns and spiritual songs. Sing and make music in your heart to the Lord, always giving thanks to God the Father for everything, in the name of our Lord Jesus Christ.
Ephesians 5:19-20 (NIV)

These verses prove just how much music is a powerful tool. Music has the ability to speak to the heart and to encourage those who are in a bad place that words alone cannot do. Yet, we have that chance to soften someone's heart and give them the hope of Christ through something as simple as a song. In addition, we are given the mandate to praise God and give Him thanks for everything in the name of Jesus. Worship leading allows us to do exactly that.

BEHIND THE WORSHIP

_____
_____
_____
_____
_____
_____
_____
_____
_____
_____
_____
_____
_____
_____
_____
_____
_____
_____
_____
_____
_____
_____
_____
_____
_____
_____
_____
_____
_____
_____
_____
_____
_____
_____
_____
_____.

DAY 2

God is spirit, and his worshipers must worship in the Spirit and in truth.

John 4:24 (NIV)

Worship is to be done in Spirit and truth. The songs should provide the truth. Yet, to truly and effectively minister, it's imperative that the Spirit is ministering to and through you, the worship leader.

This means that as a worship leader, your life must be one of the truth that you sing about. The workings of the Spirit of God must be evident in the life you live. When it is time to lead others, being full of God and His spirit, it's inevitable that your worship will reflect and display what God has done or is doing in your life. The truth is made believable by the freedom of the Spirit.

BEHIND THE WORSHIP

_____

_____

_____

_____

_____

_____

_____

_____

_____

_____

_____

_____

_____

_____

_____

_____

_____

_____

_____

_____

_____

_____

_____

_____

_____

_____

_____

_____

_____

_____

_____.

DAY 3

As a prisoner for the Lord, then, I urge you to live a life worthy of the calling you have received.

Ephesians 4:1 (NIV)

We've been called to lead worship at such a time as this. Ministry is a gift, and an undeserving opportunity the Lord chose to give us, in setting the atmosphere and preparing the way for the word He has spoken.

Therefore, as a great calling and gift, our lives should reflect what and why you sing every day in and out of church. The goal is to never give God a reason to take it away or give it to someone else because we didn't take it serious enough – or rather, we didn't live a life worthy of such an awesome calling.

_____
_____
_____
_____
_____
_____
_____
_____
_____
_____
_____
_____
_____
_____
_____
_____
_____
_____
_____
_____
_____
_____
_____
_____
_____
_____
_____
_____
_____
_____
_____
_____
_____
_____
_____ .

DAY 4

In the year that King Uzziah died, I saw the Lord,
high and exalted, seated on a throne; and the train of
his robe filled the temple.

Isaiah 6:1 (NIV)

King Uzziah distracted Isaiah from seeing God. Once the hindrance died, his eyes were opened. Isaiah regained focus on the Lord. Likewise, we are challenged to see what may be hindering us from full fellowship with God.

Even on a smaller scale, we must ask ourselves: What is disabling the productiveness and spiritual efficiency of ministry? Someone once described it as "scattered minds." Too many times, whether in rehearsal, leading worship, or in our own lives, we lose sight of God and what He is teaching us or doing in those moments because we are focusing on everything else. It was Glenn Amos who said, "The devil doesn't want all your heart; he just wants enough so that God doesn't have it all." Does God have your fully undivided attention?

DAY 5

Yet I hold this against you: You have forsaken the love you had at first.

Revelation 2:4 (NIV)

A praise team is only as effective as the God working inside each member. So, the question is asked, like the church in Ephesus, have you forgotten your first love? Have you lost the enthusiasm as you would have and all you would do when you truly love someone, especially in the very beginning stages?

If you have the desire to spend time with that person and share your life with him or her, and have the tendency to share your excitement with whomever you come in contact, is that how you relate in ministering? Your excitement and enthusiasm of Christ is your love for Him, His deep love for you, and what He's done for you. Does it show in your worship? Or are you just playing a part?

_____
_____
_____
_____
_____
_____
_____
_____
_____
_____
_____
_____
_____
_____
_____
_____
_____
_____
_____
_____
_____
_____
_____
_____
_____
_____
_____
_____
_____
_____.

DAY 6

What is mankind that you are mindful of them,
human beings that you care for them?
                                    Psalms 8:4 (NIV)

It's that "ah-ha moment" when you realize who God is
and who we are in comparison. It really makes you wonder
why and how He could really love us. When you finally
grasp that concept, your praise and worship must reflect
that wonder. Likewise, you should love and strive to live
for Him even more, because He didn't have to love you,
let alone die for you, but He did.

There is nothing about us that gives God a reason to love
and care for us in the way He does. Like the song says,
"Not because of who I am, but because of what You've
done. Not because of what I've done, but because of who
You are" ("Who Am I," Casting Crowns). That's enough
to praise Him.

_____

_____

_____

_____

_____

_____

_____

_____

_____

_____

_____

_____

_____

_____

_____

_____

_____

_____

_____

_____

_____

_____

_____

_____

_____

_____

_____

_____

_____

_____

_____

_____

_____

_____.

DAY 7

His master replied, "Well done, good and faithful servant! You have been faithful with a few things; I will put you in charge of many things. Come and share your master's happiness!"

Matthew 25:21 (NIV)

Serve wholeheartedly, as if you were serving the Lord, not people, [8] because you know that the Lord will reward each one for whatever good they do, whether they are slave or free.

Ephesians 6:7-8 (NIV)

We live in a time where commitment and dedication are short lived; once we get tired or find something new to use up our time, we run. In the same way, people say they want to be a part of something, but only on their terms. Yet, in the parable of the talents, the master blessed the servants, because even with the little they had, they stayed faithful.

In the same way, God will bless our faithfulness to the work He has assigned for us to do in this lifetime. Even to the church in Ephesus, Paul encouraged them to put their whole heart into whatever they did – no half-stepping – and to give all they had as if God signed their checks. Thus, like the good servant, commitment and a faithful heart in ministry, no matter how frustrating, tiring, strenuous, or seemingly pointless it can be, will surely be rewarded.

_____

_____

_____

_____

_____

_____

_____

_____

_____

_____

_____

_____

_____

_____

_____

_____

_____

_____

_____

_____

_____

_____

_____

_____

_____

_____

_____

_____

_____ .

DAY 8

Take delight in the LORD, and he will give you your heart's desires. *⁵Commit everything you do to the LORD. Trust him, and he will help you.*

Psalm 37:4-5 (NLT)

One of the most beautiful things about the God we serve is that He wants to fulfill the prayer of Jabez in our life (1 Chron. 4:10), but that is contingent upon our relationship with Him and how we make use of the responsibility He gave us, especially as a worship leader. Whatever your desires are or wherever you feel the Lord is leading you, continually delight in Him, and His desires will become yours – and they will be far beyond your imagination (Eph. 3:20).

Though His timing and ways are vastly different than our own, as we pursue Him, He promises to bless us and open doors for us that no man can shut (Rev. 3:8). So, as this verse says, walking in obedience, commit your ways to the Lord and He will lead you in the way of the everlasting, and it will blow your mind.

BEHIND THE WORSHIP

_____

_____

_____

_____

_____

_____

_____

_____

_____

_____

_____

_____

_____

_____

_____

_____

_____

_____

_____

_____

_____

_____

_____

_____

_____

_____

_____

_____

_____

_____

_____

_____

_____

_____.

DAY 9

Our God, will you not judge them? For we have no power to face this vast army that is attacking us. We do not know what to do, but our eyes are on you... [18] *Jehoshaphat bowed down with his face to the ground, and all the people of Judah and Jerusalem fell down in worship before the* LORD. [19] *Then some Levites from the Kohathites and Korahites stood up and praised the* LORD, *the God of Israel, with a very loud voice.* [20] *Early in the morning they left for the Desert of Tekoa. As they set out, Jehoshaphat stood and said, "Listen to me, Judah and people of Jerusalem! Have faith in the* LORD *your God and you will be upheld; have faith in his prophets and you will be successful."* [21] *After consulting the people, Jehoshaphat appointed men to sing to the* LORD *and to praise him for the splendor of his holiness as they went out at the head of the army, saying: 'Give thanks to the* LORD, *for his love endures forever.'* [22] *As they began to sing and praise, the* LORD *set ambushes against the men of Ammon and Moab and Mount Seir who were invading Judah, and they were defeated."*

2 Chronicles 20:12, 18-22 (NIV)

So many times, we are faced with problems and obstacles that we have no means to overcome. Just like King Jehoshaphat and the Israelites, they were facing an enemy way out of their league. It was impossible for them to defeat their enemy alone. Yet with the prompting of their leader, they worshiped God and trusted Him to see them through. You then see that they literally praised their way out of the enemy's attacks, similar to the story of the walls of Jericho.

What's the lesson here? Use a great weapon that is oftentimes downplayed or overlooked: praise. In the midst of praising God, God Himself defeated their enemies. Praise and worship are critical; it's a defense mechanism, and by leading, you have the power to stop the enemy in his tracks.

_____

_____

_____

_____

_____

_____

_____

_____

_____

_____

_____

_____

_____

_____

_____

_____

_____

_____

_____.

DAY 10

They conquered him by the blood of the Lamb and by the word of their testimony, for they did not love their lives in the face of death.

Revelation 12:11 (HSCB)

This passage in Revelation relays the battle between the angels and demons. Satan and his angels were thrown out of Heaven onto Earth, creating Hell on Earth. However, the voice from Heaven gave an awesome hope that we already conquered him. How? Through the blood of Christ and our testimony.

When leading in worship, as a believer, whether you sing it or speak it, you are testifying about the greatness of Christ, denying yourself and edifying Him. Our testimony, in whatever format given, is another marvelous weapon that we can use to defeat Satan. Don't be afraid of your testimony. The work God has done in your life has the power to break the chains of Satan and set someone else free.

_____
_____
_____
_____
_____
_____
_____
_____
_____
_____
_____
_____
_____
_____
_____
_____
_____
_____
_____
_____
_____
_____
_____
_____
_____
_____
_____
_____
_____
_____
_____
_____
_____
_____.

DAY 11

For as I walked around and looked carefully at your objects of worship, I even found an altar with this inscription: TO AN UNKNOWN GOD. *So you are ignorant of the very thing you worship – and this is what I am going to proclaim to you.*

Acts 17:23 (MSG)

As praise and worship leaders, our duty is to proclaim who the Lord is to those we would minister. Some people are uncertain and others curious, believers included, of who God really is.

In ministering through music, we have the chance to answer that question, "Who is God?" Through the word of our testimonies, we are able to bring the light and give a response to that very pertinent question that so many are asking and starving to know. Our goal is to know God and make Him known.

_____
_____
_____
_____
_____
_____
_____
_____
_____
_____
_____
_____
_____
_____
_____
_____
_____
_____
_____
_____
_____
_____
_____
_____
_____
_____
_____
_____
_____
_____
_____
_____
_____
_____.

DAY 12

Children, don't drag your feet in this! GOD has chosen you to take your place before him to serve in conducting and leading worship – this is your life work; make sure you do it and do it well.

2 Chronicles 29:11 (MSG)

If your heart believes that God has called you to the place of a worship leader, take your place. There is nothing trivial about the matter of being a worship leader, and this matter of service to the Lord is one of the most critical. Consequently, the moment we go behind the mic, we should make music and noise that is pure and expectant of a move of God.

As humans, we have and will inevitably make mistakes. Our job is not to be the best worship singer, but rather to use our talent to foster our gift of leading people into the manifest presence of God. Take the time to practice and perfect your musical talents, as it's a part of nurturing and fulfilling God's call on your life. However you choose to lead the people, do it well and in excellence, so that the honored guest, the Living God of the universe, feels welcomed.

DAY 13

Your procession, God, has come into view, the procession of my God and King into the sanctuary. *[25] In front are the singers, after them the musicians; with them are the young women playing the timbrels.*

Psalm 68:24-25 (NIV)

Just think about it… When God wanted to come manifest His presence in the sanctuary, He chose the Levites, singers, and musicians to usher Him in. What an awesome honor that is!

It's no coincidence that most services have praise and worship at the beginning of service, because we are the ones who open the door for God to come in and move. Our place and calling is a serious and humbling thing because it sets up the hearts, eyes, and ears of those that would be a part to witness a move of God, not only through the music, but the rest of the service as well.

BEHIND THE WORSHIP

_____
_____
_____
_____
_____
_____
_____
_____
_____
_____
_____
_____
_____
_____
_____
_____
_____
_____
_____
_____
_____
_____
_____
_____
_____
_____
_____
_____
_____
_____
_____.

DAY 14

*The singers raised their voices in praise to the LORD
and sang: "He is good; his love endures forever."
Then the temple of the LORD was filled with the
cloud, [14] and the priests could not perform their service
because of the cloud, for the glory of the LORD filled
the temple of God.*

2 Chronicles 5:13b-14 (NIV)

As a worship leader, our goal should be to proclaim God
every time we stand before His people. Our hearts' desire
should be that we are able to open the doors of the Holy
of Holies and bring the people of God to the foot of the
throne of the Most High God, in such a way that the
glorious and undeniable manifestation of the Spirit of God
saturates the sanctuary. Even the thought of leaving His
awesome presence is unthinkable, for the worship
atmosphere would be so thick.

But let's be real. The chances of that happening every
single time during musical worship is slim to none, and
that's okay. Yet still, that's where our hearts should be:
cooperating in obedience to the Spirit of God, because we
have no say in God's plans nor in the willing hearts of the
people.

_____
_____
_____
_____
_____
_____
_____
_____
_____
_____
_____
_____
_____
_____
_____
_____
_____
_____
_____
_____
_____
_____
_____
_____
_____
_____
_____
_____
_____
_____
_____.

DAY 15

Let all things be done decently and in order.
1 Corinthians 14:40 (KJV)

Yeah, it can be difficult to lead worship when everyone is looking at you like you have three eyes and four ears, and they seem less engaged than you would like. You may become overwhelmed with the urge to keep pressing or even get upset and use conviction or shame to convince people to worship. Once that happens, we have already lost the battle.

There were a lot of things happening in Corinth that Paul addressed in his letter. He needed to get things straight because those of that church were creating a bad reputation for themselves. A part of that was how they worshipped, and the problem was that it caused confusion, especially to nonbelievers.

When we lead worship, our emotions are and should be involved, but our spirit has to be even more engaged, because sometimes what we want is simply not what God has in mind. Does that mean we are wrong in wanting it? Of course not! But we must be sensitive to the Spirit as well as the hearts of the people, who just may not be in a receptive place – and that is okay. As the Lord told me once, just do what He tells you to do for that particular time, and sometimes He may surprise you.

_____
_____
_____
_____
_____
_____
_____
_____
_____
_____
_____
_____
_____
_____
_____
_____
_____
_____
_____
_____
_____
_____
_____
_____
_____
_____
_____
_____
_____
_____
_____
_____
_____
_____.

DAY 16

But the priests were too few, so that they were unable to skin all the burnt offerings; therefore their brothers the Levites helped them until the work was completed and until the other priests had consecrated themselves. For the Levites were more conscientious to consecrate themselves than the priests.

2 Chronicles 29:34 (NASB)

The Levites, who had one of many responsibilities in leading the people in musical worship, were more purified than the priest – in fact, they were purified enough to do the priests' job.

Whoa. This just raises the standard of a worship leader and how we live. No, we won't be perfect Christians and we will have our bad days, but because of the task we have been given, we should be conscious and intentional about being pure and upright before God.

Our most effective ministry comes from a pure heart, but if there is a lot of junk in there that has yet to be dealt with or even acknowledged, our power and influence is limited when we lead worship. We should be known as the godliest of people, because our work directly affects the ministry as a whole. Every now and again, we need to do a spiritual detox and consecrate ourselves so that we may be aligned perfectly to the will, worship, and wonder of the Lord.

_____.

DAY 17

For the word of God is living and active and sharper than any two-edged sword, and piercing as far as the division of soul and spirit, of both joints and marrow, and able to judge the thoughts and intentions of the heart.

Hebrews 3:16 (NASB)

There are many songs out there under the Christian music umbrella. However, that does not mean that every song actually depicts the Word of God. Therefore, as a worship leader, it has to be more than the melody or the rhythm of the song or the harmonies that make us choose a song. Does the music exalt God and His Word? A beautiful tune is pleasing to the ear, but it's only the word of God that can speak to and transform the heart and soul. Thus, it is imperative to be conscious of the lyrics to the songs you choose for worship.

.

DAY 18

You're going to find that there will be times when people will have no stomach for solid teaching, but will fill up on spiritual junk food – catchy opinions that tickle their fancy. They'll turn their backs on truth and chase mirages. But you – keep your eye on what you're doing; accept the hard times along with the good; keep the Message alive; do a thorough job as God's servant.

2 Timothy 4:3 (MSG)

Plenty of people have opinions about everything; unfortunately, this is true even in the church realm. Considering the verse in Hebrews, it's the Word of God that makes the difference, yet too many in the pulpit give a watered-down gospel and execute every part of the verse in 2 Timothy.

However, it is not only in the pulpit where you hear this ear tickling, but it is also heard in many Christian songs today. As you study and connect to the True Vine, recognize the mirages that may confuse or mislead those to whom you are ministering.

_____
_____
_____
_____
_____
_____
_____
_____
_____
_____
_____
_____
_____
_____
_____
_____
_____
_____
_____
_____
_____
_____
_____
_____
_____
_____
_____
_____
_____
_____
_____
_____
_____.

DAY 19

For our struggle is not against flesh and blood, but against the rulers, against the powers, against the world forces of this darkness, against the spiritual forces of wickedness in the heavenly places.

Ephesians 4:12 (NIV)

Why is ministering the truth of the Word of God through music important? The Word of God, the sword, is the only weapon given in the armor we are mandated to put on every day. We are constantly in a battle with the enemy, as this verse explains. Even in church Satan is busy, especially when the saints gather for worship. Distraction is one of his biggest tools, whether it's what's going on outside of church or what someone looks like inside of church. How often are you distracted during worship and miss something important, a word that was meant for you?

Praise and worship are the first parts of a liturgy, so we are on the front line of the battlefield. We, worship leaders, are the first defense against any attack of the enemy to distract or block the Word of God from reaching the hearts of people to get them closer to the cross. Bottom line, as your sword is dipped in beautiful song, you have the power to ward off the enemy. Armor up.

_____
_____
_____
_____
_____
_____
_____
_____
_____
_____
_____
_____
_____
_____
_____
_____
_____
_____
_____
_____
_____
_____
_____
_____
_____
_____
_____
_____
_____
_____
_____
_____
_____
_____.

DAY 20

For everything there is a season, a time for every activity under heaven.

Ecclesiastes 3:1 (NLT)

As a matter of unity, *theme* is very significant part of worship. As much as one is able, there should be a unified message within the church or at the very least the message of a service.

It's true that there is a season for everything, including the music of worship. Within your own church, get in agreement with the pastor or ministry leaders so that where they are trying to lead the people, you can be a reaffirming guide. Recognize the season the church is in and by the Spirit of God, minister in song accordingly. This is not a matter of doctrine, but of appropriateness. Thus, pay attention to what God is leading you to play – your favorite song may not be in tune with the season or vision that the Lord gave your pastor.

_____

DAY 21

So, my dear brothers and sisters, be strong and immovable. Always work enthusiastically for the Lord, for you know that nothing you do for the Lord is ever useless.

1 Corinthians 15:58 (NLT)

Let's be honest: Leading worship can be one of the most challenging, frustrating, disappointing, and downright aggravating things you can ever do. It might be hard to stay excited during worship when it seems like you're the only one happy about praising the Lord in song, let alone worshiping in song. Bad worshipping experiences can make you feel like you are out of place. Still, you just might desire a fresh encounter with God, because the worship seems redundant. Either way, it's easy and far from uncommon to feel like your ministry is in vain.

Nevertheless, the opposite is true. As the Lord has placed you in this position, your work is not done, even if it appears you aren't making a difference. You never know whose heart and soul you are ministering to, and they may never tell you. In all you do, never lose perspective or hope in what you do as a worship leader. Unless the Lord leads you elsewhere, never lose the excitement in ushering in the presence of Almighty God, because sometimes, *you* are the person you are supposed to minister to.

_____
_____
_____
_____
_____
_____
_____
_____
_____
_____
_____
_____
_____
_____
_____
_____
_____
_____
_____
_____
_____
_____
_____
_____
_____
_____
_____
_____
_____
_____
_____
_____
_____.

DAY 22

With the tongue we praise our Lord and Father, and with it we curse human beings, who have been made in God's likeness.

James 3:9 (NIV)

This scripture should never identify you as the praise leader, but unfortunately, it proves true far too often. Some worship leaders are mean, slanderous, and or the words of their song are vastly different than the words of their everyday lives. Just as children of God, we recognize that every person was created in the image of God as the verse echoes Genesis; therefore, we should speak with grace, goodness, truth, and love every time we open our mouths (Eph. 4:25-31).

If you minister about the same principles, yet you don't live them out, something is gravely wrong. This paradox can block people from taking you seriously or entering the presence of God, because they know the type of ungodly character that dwells within you. Your ministry becomes a performance. When your life and ministry contradict one other, it is difficult for true ministry to take place. Don't be your own hindrance.

_____
_____
_____
_____
_____
_____
_____
_____
_____
_____
_____
_____
_____
_____
_____
_____
_____
_____
_____
_____
_____
_____
_____
_____
_____
_____
_____
_____
_____
_____.

DAY 23

But one time when they tried it, the evil spirit replied,
"I know Jesus, and I know Paul, but who are you?"
Acts 19:15 (NLT)

Just as others in the congregation know the real you, demons know the real you too. As said before, we are on the front line as worship leaders so we must be consecrated and equipped to disrupt the attacks of the enemy and his demons, because they are well aware of who is truly living for God and those that are out of line.

God, of course, has the ability to use even the most unworthy to accomplish His purpose; however, if the Enemy isn't scared of you, depreciating the power you have, it's safe to assume that God could be doing a lot more through you if you were truly aligned with Him. In whatever way this applies, the bottom line is to live a life so that the devil and all his demons know exactly who you are, by name.

_____

_____

_____

_____

_____

_____

_____

_____

_____

_____

_____

_____

_____

_____

_____

_____

_____

_____

_____

_____

_____

_____

_____

_____

_____

_____

_____

_____.

DAY 24

I planted, Apollos watered, but God gave the increase. ⁷ So then neither he who plants is anything, nor he who waters, but God who gives the increase.
1 Corinthians 3:6-7 (NKJV)

As a worship leader, it's common to think there is no fruit from our labor when people seem to have little desire to worship with you. Yet, I have learned that it's a matter of sheer obedience: doing what the Lord told you to do, because we have no control over how the Lord works in the heart and spirit of an individual.

Furthermore, the verse reminds us that the only thing we can do is plant or water, and the growth is up to God. Some flowers spend a lot of time underground before they sprout; others may sprout but take forever to bloom; still others we may never see the blossom. Never lose sight of what God has for you to do and where He has instructed you to go, for if you stay faithful, you will be a witness to the influence you made, in this life, the next, or both if you are so blessed.

_____

_____

_____

_____

_____

_____

_____

_____

_____

_____

_____

_____

_____

_____

_____

_____

_____

_____

_____

_____

_____

_____

_____

_____

_____

_____

_____

_____

_____

_____.

DAY 25

For if anyone thinks he is something [special] when [in fact] he is nothing [special except in his own eyes], he deceives himself. ⁴But each one must carefully scrutinize his own work [examining his actions, attitudes, and behavior], and then he can have the personal satisfaction and inner joy of doing something commendable without comparing himself to another.

Galatians 6:3-4 (AMP)

Just as it is common to be frustrated, it is also easy to fall into the detrimental trap of pride. In some churches, the worship leader is elevated and praised as the pastors, if not more, becoming haughty and egotistic.

Like how the passage in 1 Corinthians explains, God is the One who touches the hearts of the people; we are nothing more than vessels. When we look at ourselves compared to the incredible holiness of God, we recognize how unholy and unworthy we are, which drives us to be even more grateful to be used in such a way by this awesome God. He has every right and way of sitting us down and not using us. Don't deceive yourself. Examine your heart and motives constantly to verify whether they are in tune with the heart of God and His Word. If they are, praise and glorify God all the more and boast in His work in your life.

_____
_____
_____
_____
_____
_____
_____
_____
_____
_____
_____
_____
_____
_____
_____
_____
_____
_____
_____
_____
_____
_____
_____
_____
_____
_____
_____
_____
_____
_____
_____
_____
_____.

DAY 26

And David was greatly distressed; for the people spake of stoning him, because the soul of all the people was grieved, every man for his sons and for his daughters: but David encouraged himself in the LORD his God.

1 Samuel 3:0:6 (KJV)

Plenty times when worship leading, I felt closer to God than I had previously, as if my ministry were more for me than for the people. It's something about leading worship that forces you to become vulnerable before God, whether by sharing a testimony, praying, or sharing something the Lord spoke to you, even if it is a personal struggle. There are times we lead people although our own lives are broken. In these cases, we need to get before the throne of God, so we are able to face the challenges in our lives and encourage ourselves just like David. And when the people of God connect with you in those moments, it really does make it more beautiful and filling, yet humbling and comforting.

_____
_____
_____
_____
_____
_____
_____
_____
_____
_____
_____
_____
_____
_____
_____
_____
_____
_____
_____
_____
_____
_____
_____
_____
_____
_____
_____
_____
_____
_____
_____
_____
_____
_____.

DAY 27

Let the word of Christ dwell in you richly in all wisdom; teaching and admonishing one another in psalms and hymns and spiritual songs, singing with grace in your hearts to the Lord.

Colossians 3:16 (KJV)

Simply put, this mandate should be less than an issue being in music ministry, yet there are some things that we need to give attention to. For example, there are three different genres listed in this verse, and taking it at face value, there should be variety in song choice because each type of song brings a different message and serves a different purpose, all of which are needed.

As worship leaders, we should include variety in our song choices. Each of the songs we select must be chosen carefully to reflect the Lord's word, as this verse explains. The Word must be in your heart, and you must be gracious through your ministry, so that what you sing reflects your actions. This is the only way you can teach and admonish through song.

DAY 28

And do not be conformed to this world, but be transformed by the renewing of your mind, that you may prove what is that good and acceptable and perfect will of God.

Romans 12:2 (NKJV)

A lot of times there is the urge to appease the culture to attract the masses in whatever ways we can; however, there has to be a standard, whether it be in how we dress when we are ministering, the types of songs we select (such as remakes of secular songs), how we move or dance on the platform, or simply trying to be relatable in what we say. To each person there are different convictions, but in however you choose to lead the people, always bring it under the captivity of the Word of God and what He considers holy.

.

DAY 29

He must become greater; I must become less.

John 3:30 (NIV)

The more you lead, the closer the congregation should be at the face of Christ. In many cases, praise from others is inevitable, but never become such a performer that all others see is you instead of Christ. In other words, if the Holy Spirit were to leave the sanctuary for any reason, would you still be able to sing? Would the people still worship God or would it just be a grand sing-along?

Worship is not about me, nor is it about you – never has, never will. I may have the talent to sing a pretty tune, but how am I perfecting my gift to lead God's people to His feet?

_____

DAY 30

You ask [God for something] and do not receive it, because you ask with wrong motives [out of selfishness or with an unrighteous agenda], so that [when you get what you want] you may spend it on your [hedonistic] desires.

James 4:3 (AMP)

Praying is crucial to the eternal significance of any ministry, especially music. Nevertheless, what are you praying for and what are the motives behind it? Is your desire to be glorified or have your name in flashing lights or people downloading your music off of wherever? God knows our hearts, and it may seem as if people are responding well to your worship style, but are hearts really being changed? Are people just mimicking what they see you do or following what you ask them to do?

Never stop praying for the people you minister to; be sure that your desires focus on God getting all the glory, because all we do should be for His glory and His alone.

DAY 31

For the gifts and the calling of God are irrevocable.
Romans 11:29 (NKJV)

"God is the only one that can fire you and let you keep your job." There are times that God may convict us and or discipline us for sin via our actions, words, or matters of our heart that have yet to be resolved, but He continues to allow us to use our talents, though not our gifts.

This verse screams of the mercy and grace of God. No matter how far we stray or lose sight, God will not change His mind about us and what He desires to do by and through us. Even if we take the hard road by our stubbornness, all we must do is repent and let the blood of Jesus escort us back to the presence of God, manifesting Himself when we share the gifts He gave us.

_____
_____
_____
_____
_____
_____
_____
_____
_____
_____
_____
_____
_____
_____
_____
_____
_____
_____
_____
_____
_____
_____
_____
_____
_____
_____
_____
_____
_____
_____
_____
_____.

DAY 32

Therefore if anyone cleanses himself from the latter, he will be a vessel for honor, sanctified and useful for the Master, prepared for every good work.
2 Timothy 2:21 (NKJV)

For God to manifest Himself through our gifts, as was discussed prior, we must ensure that our lives are pure from the things that destroy our testimony, by word or deed (Galatians 5:19-21; 2 Timothy 2:22-24; Colossians 3:5-9; Ephesians 4:21-31). Once we are cleaned, we can be used in whatever way the Lord desires. It truly is an awesome thing to be chosen for ministry by God – never take that lightly. As messed up as we are, the Lord handpicked us to be His precious vessels for leading His people into His manifest presence.

DAY 33

²Worship the LORD with gladness; come before him with joyful songs. ⁴ Enter his gates with thanksgiving and his courts with praise; give thanks to him and praise his name.

Psalm 100:2, 4 (NIV)

How should you be when you worship? Glad. What do you bring? A joyful song. How do you bring it? With thanksgiving and praise. Doesn't get any simpler than that.

When people watch you as their worship leader, they should be looking at the face of a person who is happy to enter into the presence of God. It should be obvious that the worship leader believes every line they sing. He is worthy, and we should never allow anyone to forget that or make it a trivial matter as long as we are before them, for this is how we should start a service, joyfully entering the presence of God.

DAY 34

Do not be deceived: God cannot be mocked.
Galatians 6:7a (NIV)

Don't be mistaken: Because of the weight of our role as worship leaders, we should by no means try to pull the wool over God's eyes, if for no other reason, we can't. God knows our hearts and what we do before and after we pick up the mic. Though we may be able to put on a show in front of the people, God is not deceived. We must remember that the Lord is keeping track and our effectiveness in our ministry is contingent on our worship off the stage.

It's normal for people to be moved emotionally due to a beautiful voice, but there is something special when the Spirit of God rests upon the voice or the hands of a musician and His touch that resonates long after the song is over.

God knows if our worship is pure and when it's not, we can only assume that we will be held to a higher standard when we meet Jesus. Still, God is gracious and merciful, because we are far from perfect. There are times we fall short right before we lead the people, but don't ever be so prideful to believe the lie of Satan that God does not see you behind your "worship."

BEHIND THE WORSHIP

_____
_____
_____
_____
_____
_____
_____
_____
_____
_____
_____
_____
_____
_____
_____
_____
_____
_____
_____
_____
_____
_____
_____
_____
_____
_____
_____
_____
_____
_____
_____
_____.

DAY 35

Now the rest of the people – the priests, the Levites, the gatekeepers, the singers, the Nethinim, and all those who had separated themselves from the peoples of the lands to the Law of God, their wives, their sons, and their daughters, everyone who had knowledge and understanding – ^{29} *these joined with their brethren, their nobles, and entered into a curse and an oath to walk in God's Law, which was given by Moses the servant of God, and to observe and do all the commandments of the* LORD *our Lord, and His ordinances and His statutes.*

Nehemiah 10:28-29 (NKJV)

The musician and singers we see in this passage were set apart from the common people. In the time that they were rebuilding Jerusalem, these specific groups took God and their calling serious enough to enter into their own covenant with God. Granted, they were not thinking themselves high and mighty compared to everyone else, but rather being in a leadership role, they wanted to live worthy of their calling, and they entered into a curse to keep themselves in check while they operated in unity.

For us today, those who have a role in the liturgy of the Sunday service, we must all be joined in heart and spirit, and likewise willing to receive admonishment from each other.

DAY 36

*Therefore, whether you eat or drink, or whatever you
do, do all to the glory of God.*
                              I Corinthians 10:31 (NKJV)

In the midst of the praise and admiration from church
members and others who would hear us, it's easy to get
wrapped up in the glory, the spotlight. We often see
worship leaders take advantage of their gift, desiring only
to perform or entertain. Everyone likes to hear a
compliment or appreciation for the use of their gift, but
we must never forget to divert the glory back to God.
Even if we say "thank you" to the individual who
complimented us, say a silent prayer of thanksgiving to the
Lord to be used to minister to someone.

Remember this simple verse, and remember that
everything we do is solely for God to get the glory, no
more and no less.

_____
_____
_____
_____
_____
_____
_____
_____
_____
_____
_____
_____
_____
_____
_____
_____
_____
_____
_____
_____
_____
_____
_____
_____
_____
_____
_____
_____
_____
_____
_____
_____
_____.

DAY 37

And the special gift of ministry you received when I laid hands on you and prayed – keep that ablaze! God doesn't want us to be shy with his gifts, but bold and loving and sensible.

2 Timothy 1:6 (MSG)

The last thing you want to do is become stagnant in your gift. As you lead and minister to the people in whichever ways you are able, utilize your spiritual gift(s) in your ministry. Your talent – that is singing, playing an instrument, or any other skill – is hardly what matters for eternity's sake.

As we mature in our relationship with Christ, our gifts should be nurtured and strengthened, and the results will inevitably show. Like anything else, your gift will change and it must grow. However, if that growth makes others uncomfortable or makes you uncomfortable where you are, don't put off how the Lord is working, suppress the activity of the Spirit in your life, or be afraid. Just let the Lord lead you.

_____
_____
_____
_____
_____
_____
_____
_____
_____
_____
_____
_____
_____
_____
_____
_____
_____
_____
_____
_____
_____
_____
_____
_____
_____
_____
_____
_____
_____
_____
_____
_____
_____.

DAY 38

*If we confess our sins, he is faithful and just to forgive
us our sins and to cleanse us from all unrighteousness.*
1 John 1:9 (ESV)

The Bible tells us that our salvation is a work in progress.
Yes, once we are saved we are sealed, but every day brings
its own struggles and temptations and we must die to
ourselves daily, and still we mess up, sometimes real bad.
Don't get so prideful and self-righteous that you believe
you are perfect; God hates pride and will humble you if
necessary.

When we do fall, the Lord will not take away our gift or
deny His calling on our lives. Our sin may require a sit
down, but the Lord is a restorer and with a repentant
heart, He promises to forgive us, and when He does, His
Word says that as far as the east is from the west our sins
are removed from His memory. Take joy in the mercy of
Jesus and know that we are made righteous through the
blood of His Son.

_____
_____
_____
_____
_____
_____
_____
_____
_____
_____
_____
_____
_____
_____
_____
_____
_____
_____
_____
_____
_____
_____
_____
_____.

DAY 39

For if you remain silent at this time, relief and deliverance for the Jews will arise from another place, but you and your father's family will perish. And who knows but that you have come to your royal position for such a time as this?

Esther 4:14 (NIV)

Recognize the greatness of who the Lord created you to be. He raised you up in this generation to minister to His bride, the Church. And yes, you answered the call, but maybe the Lord wants to expand and do more through you. He is patient, but like Mordecai told his cousin, the Lord may end up giving His work to another who will trust and obey, and keep saying "yes."

Don't let anyone take your position. You were made for this! You are a part of a royal priesthood; we are in a royal position and the Lord has an amazing plan and purpose in how and why He gifted you in this way. Therefore, our duty is to those of this time to bring in deliverance and relief from the darkness of this world.

DAY 40

For God so loved the world, that he gave his only begotten Son, that whosoever believeth in him should not perish, but have everlasting life.

John 3:16 (KJV)

Therefore, God elevated him to the place of highest honor and gave him the name above all other names, ¹⁰ that at the name of Jesus every knee should bow, in heaven and on earth and under the earth, ¹¹ and every tongue declare that Jesus Christ is Lord, to the glory of God the Father.

Philippians 2:9-11 (NLT)

Look, I am coming soon, bringing my reward with me to repay all people according to their deeds. ¹³ I am the Alpha and the Omega, the First and the Last, the Beginning and the End.

Revelation 22:12-13

This is what it is all about. As worship leaders, we have to remember that our duty is to spotlight the cross and to help the people of God rehearse for when we see Jesus face to face and worship at His feet. We will all have to bow, but if we can help lead the people to do it now, Heaven will be so much better. Jesus is coming back, and He knows how we as worship leaders used our gift, how we answered our calling, and our motives behind it. He will repay us accordingly.

Remember that although our mission field is in part behind the microphone, we must have an intentional worship before the song, and there must be a true relationship behind the worship, for we have the greatest love story to tell through our various styles, genres, lyrical themes, and melodies. Make sure you remember why we do what we do, because it matters immensely for eternity's sake.

Made in the USA
Middletown, DE
03 September 2017